POOR RICHARD'S
ALMANACK

Benjamin Franklin

Wit and Wisdom from Poor Richard's Almanack

Steve Martin

SERIES EDITOR

Introduction by Dave Barry

THE MODERN LIBRARY

NEW YORK

2000 Modern Library Paperback Edition

Series introduction copyright © 2000 by Steve Martin
Introduction copyright © 2000 by Dave Barry

LIBRARY OF CONGRESS CATALOGING-IN-PUBLICATION DATA
Franklin, Benjamin, 1706–1790.
[Poor Richard. Selections]
Poor Richard's almanack/by Benjamin Franklin.—2000 Modern Library
paperback ed.
p. cm.
ISBN 0-679-64038-X
I. Title.
PS749.A6   2000
818'.102–dc21   99-86613

Modern Library website address: www.modernlibrary.com

Printed in the United States of America

2 4 6 8 9 7 5 3 1

BENJAMIN FRANKLIN

Benjamin Franklin—the statesman, philosopher, and man of letters who invented, among other things, American humor—was born in Boston on January 17, 1706. The tenth son of a candlemaker, he briefly attended grammar school but was largely self-taught. At the age of twelve he was apprenticed as a printer's assistant to his older brother James, who later founded the *New England Courant*. Franklin's inimitable wit first surfaced with a series of satirical letters anonymously submitted to the *Courant* in 1722. Posing as Silence Dogood, the widow of a rural clergyman who admits a "natural Inclination to observe and reprove the Faults of others," he inveighed against the immodesty of hoop petticoats, reproached drunkenness, questioned the value of a Harvard education, and lampooned the New England funeral elegy while offering a satirical recipe for composing one. Written in a colloquial style inspired by *The Spectator* of Addison and Steele, the Dogood papers proved enormously popular with readers. Franklin visited London for a time following government suppression of the *Courant* but eventually settled in Philadelphia. In 1729 he acquired the *Pennsylvania Gazette* and later used it to publish America's first newspaper cartoons. Over the next decades he devoted himself tirelessly to public service and devised numerous inventions, including bifocal spectacles, a rocking chair that fanned as it rocked, and the Franklin stove. His famous scientific studies culminated in the publication of *Experiments and Observations on Electricity* in 1751.

During this period Franklin enjoyed enormous success with *Poor Richard's Almanack*. He first published it in 1732, when he was only twenty-six, and continued with new editions annually for the next quarter century, often selling as many as ten thousand copies each year. Surpassed in sales only by the Bible, the *Almanack* provided Franklin with considerable wealth and fame. Adopting the persona of Richard Saunders, a dreamy astrologer and sometime moralist whose wife urges him to think of his familial responsibility, he offered up everything from weather predictions and horoscopes to commonsense observations and wise saws. Though the maxims, epigrams, and proverbs that fill the pages of *Poor Richard's Almanack* were often borrowed from Rabelais, Dryden, Pope, Swift, Sterne, and other masters, Franklin delivered them in a fresh and authentic voice that helped define American humor. It is widely held that his writing heralded Mark

Twain, and critic Malcolm Cowley deemed Franklin "the first truly effective American prose writer."

Franklin devoted much of his later life to diplomatic service abroad. He traveled to England in 1757 as an agent of the Pennsylvania Assembly and spent most of the next eighteen years in London representing the American colonies in disputes about taxation that culminated in the Revolution. "An Edict by the King of Prussia" (1773), a clever satire of burdensome British trade regulations, exemplifies Franklin's use of humor to undercut his opponents. After returning home in 1775 Franklin helped draft the Declaration of Independence, though reportedly the other Founding Fathers did not trust him to write the proclamation for fear he might put a joke in it. When the document was signed he supposedly quipped to John Hancock: "We must indeed all hang together, or most assuredly we shall all hang separately." In 1776 Franklin went back to Europe as ambassador to France, where he was lionized by Parisian society, and subsequently negotiated the Treaty of Paris that ended the American Revolution. His wit ever intact, Franklin amused himself by writing a series of lighthearted, satirical essays known as the *Bagatelles,* the most famous of which are "The Morals of Chess," "The Ephemera," and "Dialogue Between the Gout and Mr. Franklin." In 1785 he left Europe for the last time. Benjamin Franklin completed his now classic *Autobiography* in 1789 and died in Philadelphia on April 17, 1790.

Introduction to the Modern Library Humor and Wit Series

Steve Martin

When I was asked to be the editor for the Modern Library Humor series, including books that had been written as far back as the mid-eighteenth century, I was shocked. I frankly was not aware that anything funny had been written before I started writing. I had indeed heard of S. J. Perelman, James Thurber, and the like, but I was also aware that they were heavily influenced by me, even lifting some of my ideas, backdating them, and carefully inserting them in magazines from the thirties with the clever use of a razor blade and glue.

That said, I have read the essays in the Modern Library's editions, and will give these authors credit in that they have been extremely nimble in adapting my ideas—for example, my use of the word "the" before nouns—and disguising it so there appears to be no plagiarism at all.

Unlike as in most of the arts, greatness in comedy is not necessarily judged by its ability to transcend generations. Comedy is designed to make people laugh now, not three generations later, and it would be a poor stand-up comedian who suggested waiting forty-five years for a joke to take hold. Have you ever seen cartoons from early-twentieth-century magazines? The ones with captions that are longer than the phone book?

> "Eloise, it seems to me that the men should retire to the den for sport and that the ladies should remain in the dining area until that hour which it is deemed appropriate for the..." blah blah blah

What were they laughing at?

But just because it isn't funny now doesn't mean it wasn't funny then. And, even though you have probably burst into uncontrollable fits of hysteria several times already in the reading of this essay, that doesn't mean that this will be hilariously funny *one thousand years from now*.

In fact, I worry that my fantasy dinner party, at which Mark Twain, Benjamin Franklin, S. J. Perelman, and Nora Ephron hold court in my dining room, instead of being from-mouth-to-page publishable, might be a disaster. Would Ben utter a short, to-the-point epigram, Twain offer a witticism, Perelman deliver an exasperated self-deprecation, and Ephron observe a social irony, and then all of them sit there, separated by generations, wondering what the others were talking about?

So in choosing the books for this series, it was necessary to select works whose humor remains intact for us today. Generally, the ability for humor to last is explained away by saying that it appeals to something in us that is human and universal. This is a cheap, dopey explanation, and I'm upset that you suggested it. I prefer to think that transcendent humor is the product of funny people, and that's all there is to say. Who would you rather have at your party, someone human and universal, or someone who is deeply funny? This is why my fantasy dinner party would be swell, because all of these writers are deeply funny people. Although I must add that I know Nora Ephron personally, and I'm happy to say that she is also universal.

Sometimes, when I am feeling insecure about my chosen profession, I try to imagine a world without comedy—for example, the world that ducks live in. Try to imagine a political climate where an ironic comment is *seized upon by a humorless news media*. Or the world of entertainment minus the hilarious zing of celebrity interviews. It would be a sad, straight, strict world. Instead, we live in a world that is actually thriving on humor, and consuming it at an alarming rate. Comedy writers, who undoubtedly wake up in the morning with joy on their faces and a joke in their hearts, are more in demand than ever, partially because of their high suicide rate.

I suppose some kind of deeper commentary about humor is in order. I am overjoyed at the prospect of offering my very sophisticated views on humor, as I have been in the comedy world for over... wait a minute. I am suddenly reminded of a phrase that circulates around my group of funny friends, which is generally expressed thus: The day you start analyzing humor is the day you cease to be funny. I think I'd rather be funny.

Good night.

INTRODUCTION

Dave Barry

I have to admit that, when I was a youngster in grade school, I did not care for Benjamin Franklin. Teachers were always shoving him down my throat—him and his wise adages, such as "A penny saved is a penny earned." I had *no* idea what that meant.

As an adult, I see the point Franklin was making with the penny adage, but I have trouble applying it to life in the 2000s. A more accurate adage for today would be: "A penny saved is a penny that winds up in an overflowing jar of pennies that you don't want to throw away, because theoretically they are money, but you can't really *use* them as money unless you put them into coin wrappers and take them to the bank, and who has coin wrappers anyway, let alone time to be sitting around wrapping coins, and why the hell does the government even *make* pennies, anyway?"

Along the same lines: I firmly believe that early to bed, and early to rise, makes a man miss pretty much everything good on TV.

So if you want the brutal truth, I did not expect to get much useful information out of *Poor Richard's Almanack*. I wondered, what could Benjamin Franklin—a guy who has been, no offense, dead for more than two hundred years—possibly have to say that would be relevant to a resident of today's dot-com world?

Plenty, as it turns out. Now, I'm not saying that every adage in the *Almanack* rings with timeless wisdom. There are some I don't get at all. Take, for example, this one, from the 1749 *Almanack:*

If your head is wax, don't walk in the Sun.

This *sounds* vaguely wise, but I can't figure out what it means—unless it means that you should not walk around in the sun if your head is literally made out of wax, in which case my reaction is, duh. I suspect that this might be a case where Franklin couldn't come up with a legitimate adage, so he just made up something that had a kind of adag-y feel to it, like:

Celery makes a poor horse whip.

Or:

A dog that eats cheese never needs a canoe.

But I have to say, much of what I read in the *Almanack* had me nodding in agreement and wishing that modern people (including me) followed its precepts. Poor Richard advocates diligence, self-reliance, frugality, and honesty; he disdains laziness, extravagance, pretense, and immodesty. It goes without saying that he hates lawyers.

This is the ultimate self-help book, containing more practical advice on getting successfully though life than you'll hear in a thousand years of talk-show psychobabble.

You want a diet plan? Listen to Poor Richard:

To lengthen thy life, lessen thy meals.

You want good relationships?

Love and be loved.

You want to know exactly what's wrong with televangelists?

To be proud of Virtue, is to poison yourself with the Antidote.

You want to know how to be satisfied with your lot in a world where twenty-two-year-olds become Internet billionaires?

To be content, look backward on those who possess less than yourself, not forward on those who possess more. If this does not make you content, you don't deserve to be happy.

Poor Richard's Almanack isn't only wise: It's funny. In fact, the first edition of the *Almanack,* for 1733, began with a fine gag. In the preface, "Poor Richard" declared, with much mock solemnity and sorrow, that, according to his calculations, a competing almanack publisher, Titan Leeds, would die on October 17 of that year. This forced Leeds, the following year, to preface *his* Almanack with a detailed and very serious denial that he was dead. Almanack wars!

My favorite example of Franklin's humor appears in the 1757 *Almanack,* where he explains, in considerable detail, how to construct a "Striking Sundial." This is a sundial that tells the time by using the rays of the sun, magnified by lenses, to *set off cannons.* Yes! So, for example, if you heard ten cannons go off, you'd know it was ten o'clock (either that or a war had started). With this device, states the *Almanack,* "not only a Man's own Family, but all his Neighbours for ten Miles round, may know what a Clock it is, when the Sun shines. . . ."

Of course Franklin was kidding. He was using the Striking Sundial to make the point that some things cost far too much for the benefits they provide (can you say "federal government?").

I'm not saying this book is going to have you slapping your thighs all the way through. But I bet it gives you more than a few chuckles. You might even find yourself taking some of Poor Richard's advice and profiting from it. I hope you do, although I feel compelled to tell you, Courteous Reader, that if the profit is in the form of pennies, you might as well just throw them away.

In 1732, I first published my Almanack under the name of "Richard Saunders"; it was continued by me about twenty-five years, and commonly called "Poor Richard's Almanack". I endeavored to make it both entertaining and useful, and it accordingly came to be in such demand that I reaped considerable profit from it; vending annually near ten thousand. And observing that it was generally read, (scarce any neighborhood in the province being without it,) I considered it as a proper vehicle for conveying instruction among the common people, who bought scarcely any other books. I therefore filled all the little spaces that occurred between the remarkable days in the Calendar, with proverbial sentences, chiefly such as inculcated industry and frugality, as the means of procuring wealth, and thereby securing virtue; it being more difficult for a man in want to act always honestly, as (to use here one of those proverbs) "it is hard for an empty sack to stand upright." These proverbs, which contained the wisdom of many ages and nations, I assembled and formed into a connected discourse prefixed to the Almanack of 1757, as the harangue of a wise old man to the people attending an auction: the bringing all these scattered counsels thus into a focus, enabled them to make greater impression. The piece being universally approved, was copied in all the newspapers of the American Continent, reprinted in Britain on a large sheet of paper to be stuck up in houses; two translations were made of it in France, and great numbers bought by the clergy and gentry, to distribute gratis among their poor parishioners and tenants. In Pennsylvania, as it discouraged useless expense in foreign superfluities, some thought it had its share of influence in producing that growing plenty of money which was observable for several years after its publication.

—BENJAMIN FRANKLIN.

February hath XXVIII Days.

	D.	H.
New ☽	5	12 aft.
First Q.	12	9 aft.
Full ●	21	3 mor.
Last Q.	28	8 aft.

☊ { 1 ♑ 29 Deg.
11 28
21 28

Planets Places.

D.	☉	♄	♃	♂	♀	☿	☽'s L
	♒	♏	♓	♐	♑	♓	
1	24	21	2	2	24	2	S. 3
6	29	21	4	5	♒ 1	12	N. 3
11	♓ 4	21	5	7	7	20	5
16	9	21	6	10	13	27	1
21	14	21	7	13	19	♈ 1	S. 4
26	19	21	8	15	25	2	5

D	☽ rise	☽ sou.	
1	2 57	7 29	10
2	3 50	8 32	11
3	4 43	9 34	12
4	Moon	10 32	1
5	sets	11 30	2
6	A.	A. 23	3
7	7 38	1 16	4
8	8 51	2 7	5
9	10 3	2 57	5
10	11 18	3 49	6
11	12 29	4 42	7
12	M. 29	5 33	8
13	1 26	6 25	9
14	2 17	7 17	10
15	3 8	8 8	11
16	3 49	9 57	12
17	4 25	9 46	12
18	4 57	10 31	1
19	Moon	11 16	2
20	rises	11 57	2
21	A.	12 38	3
22	7 27	M. 38	3
23	8 24	1 16	4
24	9 22	1 28	4
25	10 33	2 40	5
26	11 43	3 38	6
27	12 48	4 36	7
28	M. 48	5 29	8

On the 18th of this month, *anno* 1546 died that famous reformer, LUTHER: who ſtruck the great blow to papal tyranny in *Europe*. He was remarkably *temperate* in meat and drink, ſometimes faſting four days together; and at other times, for many days, eating only a little bread and a herring. *Cicero* ſays, *There was never any* great *man who was not an* induſtrious *man*; to which may, perhaps, be added, *There was never any* induſtrious *man who was not a* temperate *man*: For intemperance in diet, abates the vigour, and dulls the action both of mind and body.

Of SOUND.

Mr. *Flamſtead*, Dr. *Halley* and Mr. *Derham*, agree that ſound moves 1142 feet in a ſecond, which is one *Engliſh* mile in 4 ſeconds and 5 8ths; that it moves in the ſame time in every different ſtate of the atmoſphere; that winds hardly make any difference in its velocity; that a languid or loud ſound moves with the ſame velocity; and that different kinds of ſounds, as of bells, guns, &c. have the ſame velocity, and are equally ſwift in the beginning as end of their motion.

Poor Richard, 1733.

A N

Almanack

For the Year of Chrift

1733,

Being the Firſt after LEAP YEAR:

And makes ſince the Creation	Years
By the Account of the Eastern *Greeks*	7241
By the Latin Church, when ☉ ent. ♈	6932
By the Computation of *W. W.*	5742
By the *Roman* Chronology	5682
By the *Jewish* Rabbies	5494

Wherein is contained

The Lunations, Eclipſes, Judgment of the Weather, Spring Tides, Planets Motions & mutual Aſpects, Sun and Moon's Riſing and Setting, Length of Days, Time of High Water, Fairs, Courts, and obſervable Days.

Fitted to the Latitude of Forty Degrees, and a Meridian of Five Hours Weſt from *London*, but may without ſenſible Error, ſerve all the adjacent Places, even from *Newfoundland* to *South-Carolina.*

By *RICHARD SAUNDERS*, Philom.

PHILADELPHIA:
Printed and ſold by *B. FRANKLIN*, at the New Printing-Office near the Market.

COURTEOUS READER,

I might in this place attempt to gain thy favour by declaring that I write Almanacks with no other view than that of the publick good, but in this I should not be sincere; and men are now a-days too wise to be deceiv'd by pretences, how specious soever. The plain truth of the matter is, I am excessive poor, and my wife, good woman, is, I tell her, excessive proud; she cannot bear, she says, to sit spinning in her shift of tow, while I do nothing but gaze at the stars; and has threatened more than once to burn all my books and rattling-traps, (as she calls my instruments,) if I do not make some profitable use of them for the good of my family. The printer has offer'd me some considerable share of the profits, and I have thus began to comply with my dame's desire.

Indeed, this motive would have had force enough to have made me publish an Almanack many years since, had it not been overpowered by my regard for my good friend and fellow-student, Mr. *Titan Leeds*, whose interest I was extreamly unwilling to hurt. But this obstacle (I am far from speaking it with pleasure,) is soon to be removed, since inexorable death, who was never known to respect merit, has already prepared the mortal dart, the fatal sister has already extended her destroying shears, and that ingenious man must soon be taken from us. He dies, by my calculation, made at his request, on Oct. 17, 1733, 3 ho., 29 m., P.M., at the very instant of the ♂ of ☉ and ☿. By his own calculation he will survive till the 26th of the same month. This small difference between us we have disputed whenever we have met these nine years past; but at length he is inclinable to agree with my judgment. Which of us is most exact, a little time will now determine. As, therefore, these Provinces may not longer expect to see any of his performances after this year I think myself free to take up the task, and request a share of publick encouragement, which I am the more apt to hope for on this account, that the buyer of my Almanack may consider himself not only as purchasing an useful utensil, but as performing an act of charity to his poor

Friend and servant,
R. SAUNDERS.*

* Titan Leeds, in his "American Almanack" for 1734, thus replies:

"Kind Reader, Perhaps it may be expected that I should say something concerning an Almanack printed for the Year 1733, Said to be writ by Poor Richard or Richard Saunders, who for want of other matter was pleased to tell his Readers, that he had calculated my Nativity, and from thence predicts my Death to be the 17th of October, 1733. At 22 min. past 3 a-Clock in the Afternoon, and that these Provinces may not expect to see any more of his (*Titan Leeds*) Performances, and this precise Predicter, who predicts to a Minute, proposes to succeed me in Writing of Almanacks; but notwithstanding his false Prediction, I have by the Mercy of God lived to write a Diary for the Year 1734, and to publish the Folly and Ignorance of this presumptuous Author. Nay, he adds another gross Falsehood in his said Almanack, viz—*That by my own Calculation, I shall survive until the 26th of the said Month,* (October) which is as untrue as the former, for I do not pretend to that Knowledge, altho' he has usurpt the Knowledge of the Almighty herein, and manifested himself a Fool and a Lyar. And by the mercy of God I have lived to survive this conceited Scriblers Day and Minute

FEBRUARY

N.N. of B——s county, pray don't be angry with poor Richard.

Each age of men new fashions doth invent;
    Things which are old, young men do not esteem:
What pleas'd our fathers, doth not us content;
    What flourished then, we out of fashion deem:
        And that's the reason, as I understand,
        Why Prodigus did sell his father's land.

———

Light purse, heavy heart.

He's a fool that makes his doctor his heir.

Ne'er take a wife till thou hast a house (and a fire) to put her in.

He's gone, and forgot nothing but to say farewell to his creditors.

Love well, whip well.

———————

whereon he has predicted my Death; and as I have supplyed my Country with Al-manacks for three seven Years by past, to general Satisfaction, so perhaps I may live to write when his Performances are Dead. *Thus much from your annual Friend, Titan Leeds, October 18, 1733, 3. ho. 33 min. P.M.*"

MARCH

My love and I for kisses play'd,
    She would keep stakes, I was content,
But when I won, she would be paid,
    This made me ask her what she meant:
        Quoth she, since you are in this wrangling vein
        Here take your kisses, give me mine again.

—

Let my respected friend J. G.
Accept this humble verse of me,
Viz.: Ingenious, learned, envy'd youth,
Go on as thou'st began;
Even thy enemies take pride,
That thou'rt their countryman.
Hunger never saw bad bread.

APRIL

Kind Katherine to her husband kiss'd these words,
  "Mine own sweet Will, how dearly I love thee!"
If true (quoth Will) the world no such affords.
  And that its true I durst his warrant be:
    For ne'er heard I of woman good or ill,
    But always loved best, her own sweet Will.

———

Great talkers, little doers.

A rich rogue is like a fat hog, who never does good
till as dead as a log.

Relation without friendship, friendship without
power, power without will, will without effect, effect
without profit, and profit without virtue, are not worth
a farto.

MAY

Mirth pleaseth some, to others 't is offence,
Some commend plain conceit, some profound sense;
Some wish a witty jest, some dislike that,
And most would have themselves they know not what.
Then he that would please all, and himself too,
Takes more in hand than he is like to do.

—

The favour of the great is no inheritance.

Fools make feasts, and wise men eat them.

Beware of the young doctor and the old barber.

He has chang'd his one ey'd horse for a blind one.

The poor have little, beggars none; the rich too
much, enough, not one.

Eat to live, and not live to eat.

JUNE

"Observe the daily circle of the sun,
And the short year of each revolving moon:
By them thou shalt foresee the following day,
Nor shall a starry night thy hopes betray.
When first the moon appears, if then she shrouds
Her silver crescent, tip'd with sable clouds,
Conclude she bodes a tempest on the main,
And brews for fields impetuous floods of rain."

—

After three days men grow weary of a wench, a guest, and weather rainy.

To lengthen thy life, lessen thy meals.

The proof of gold is fire; the proof of woman, gold; the proof of man, a woman.

After feasts made, the maker scratches his head.

JULY

"Ev'n while the reaper fills his greedy hands,
And binds the golden sheafs in brittle bands,
Oft have I seen a sudden storm arise
From all the warring winds that sweep the skies:
And oft whole sheets descend of slucy rain,
Suck'd by the spungy clouds from off the main;
The lofty skies at once come pouring down,
The promis'd crop and golden labors drown."

—

Many estates are spent in the getting,

Since women for tea forsook spinning and knitting.

He that lieth down with dogs, shall rise up with fleas.

A fat kitchen, a lean will.

Distrust and caution are the parents of security.

Tongue double, brings trouble.

AUGUST

"For us thro' twelve bright signs Apollo guides
The year, and earth in sev'ral climes divides.
Five girdles bind the skies, the torrid zone
Glows with the passing and repassing sun.
Far on the right and left, th' extreams of heav'n,
To frosts, and snows, and bitter blasts are giv'n.
Betwixt the midst and these, the gods assign'd
Two habitable seats for humane kind."

—

Take counsel in wine, but resolve afterwards in water.

He that drinks fast, pays slow.

Great famine when wolves eat wolves.

A good wife lost, is God's gift lost.

A taught horse, and a woman to teach, and teachers practising what they preach.

He is ill clothed that is bare of virtue.

SEPTEMBER

Death is a fisherman, the world we see
His fish-pond is, and we the fishes be;
His net some general sickness; howe'er he
Is not so kind as other fishers be;
For if they take one of the smaller fry,
They throw him in again, he shall not die:
But death is sure to kill all he can get,
And all is fish with him that comes to net.

—

Men and melons are hard to know.

He's the best physician that knows the worthlessness of the most medicines.

Beware of meat twice boil'd, and an old foe reconcil'd.

A fine genius in his own country, is like gold in the mine.

There is no little enemy.

The heart of the fool is in his mouth, but the mouth of the wise man is in his heart.

OCTOBER

Time was my spouse and I could not agree,
Striving about superiority:
The text which saith that man and wife are one,
Was the chief argument we stood upon:
She held, they both one woman should become;
I held they should be man, and both but one.
Thus we contended daily, but the strife
Could not be ended, till both were one wife.

—

The old man has given all to his son.

O fool! to undress thy self before thou art going to bed.

Cheese and salt meat should be sparingly eat.

Doors and walls are fools paper.

Anoint a villain and he'll stab you, stab him, and he'll anoint you.

Keep your mouth wet, feet dry.

He has lost his boots, but sav'd his spurs.

NOVEMBER

My neighbour H——y by his pleasing tongue,
Hath won a girl that's rich, wise, fair, and young;
The match (he saith) is half concluded, he
Indeed is wondrous willing; but not she,
And reason good, for he has run thro' all
Almost the story of the prodigal;
Yet swears he never with the hogs did dine;
That's true, for none would trust him with their swine.

———

Where bread is wanting, all's to be sold.

There is neither honour nor gain got in dealing with a vil-lain.

The fool hath made a vow, I guess,

Never to let the fire have peace.

Snowy winter, a plentiful harvest.

Nothing more like a fool, than a drunken man.

DECEMBER

She that will eat her breakfast in her bed,
And spend the morn in dressing of her head,
And sit at dinner like a maiden bride,
And talk of nothing all day but of pride;
God in his mercy may do much to save her,
But what a case is he in that shall have her.

———

God works wonders now and then;
Behold! a lawyer, an honest man.

He that lives carnally, won't live eternally.

Innocence is its own defence.

Time eateth all things, could old poets say,
The times are chang'd, our times *drink* all away.

Never mind it, she'l be sober after the holidays.

The Benefit of Going to Law

Dedicated to the Countess of K—t and H-n-r-d-n

Two beggars travelling along,
    One blind, the other lame.
Pick'd up an oyster on the way,
    To which they both laid claim:
The matter rose so high, that they
    Resolv'd to go to law,
As often richer fools have done,
    Who quarrel for a straw.
A lawyer took it straight in hand,
    Who knew his business was
To mind nor one nor t'other side,
    But make the best o' th' cause,
As always in the law's the case;
    So he his judgment gave,
And lawyer-like he thus resolv'd
    What each of them should have;
        Blind plaintif, lame defendant, share
        The friendly laws impartial care,
        A shell for him, a shell for thee,
        The middle is the *lawyer's fee.*

Note, This ALMANACK us'd to contain but 24 Pages, now has 36 ; yet the Price is very little advanc'd.

Poor RICHARD improved :

BEING AN

ALMANACK

AND

EPHEMERIS

OF THE

MOTIONS of the SUN and MOON;

THE TRUE

PLACES and ASPECTS of the PLANETS ;

THE

RISING and *SETTING* of the *SUN;*

AND THE

Rising, Setting *and* Southing *of the* Moon,

FOR THE

YEAR of our LORD 1749.

Containing also,

The Lunations, Conjunctions, Eclipses, Judgment of the Weather, Rising and Setting of the Planets, Length of Days and Nights, Fairs, Courts, Roads, &c. Together with useful Tables, chronological Observations, and entertaining Remarks.

Fitted to the Latitude of Forty Degrees, and a Meridian of near five Hours West from *London* ; but may, without sensible Error, serve all the NORTHERN-COLONIES.

By *RICHARD SAUNDERS,* Philom.

PHILADELPHIA:
Printed and Sold by B. FRANKLIN, and D. HALL.
G. De C. E.

JANUARY

Advice to Youth

First, Let the Fear of Him who form'd thy Frame,
Whose Hand sustain'd thee e'er thou hadst a Name,
Who brought thee into Birth, with Pow'r of Thought
Receptive of immortal Good, be wrought
Deep in thy Soul. His, not thy own, thou art;
To him resign the Empire of thy Heart.
His Will, thy Law; His Service, thy Employ;
His Frown, thy Dread, his Smile be all thy Joy.
Wealth and Content are not always Bed-fellows.
Wise Men learn by others harms; Fools by their own.

FEBRUARY

Wak'd by the Call of Morn, on early Knee,
Ere the World thrust between thy God and thee,
Let thy pure Oraisons, ascending, gain
His Ear, and Succour of his Grace obtain,
In Wants, in Toils, in Perils of the Day,
And strong Temptations that beset thy Way.
Thy best Resolves then in his Strength renew
To walk in Virtue's Paths, and Vice eschew.

———

The end of Passion is the beginning of Repentance.

Words may shew a man's Wit, but Actions his
Meaning.

MARCH

To HIM intrust thy Slumbers, and prepare
The fragrant Incense of thy Ev'ning Prayer.
But first tread back the Day, with Search severe,
And *Conscience,* chiding or applauding, hear.
Review each Step; *Where, acting, did I err?*
Omitting, where? Guilt either Way infer.
Labour this Point, and while thy Frailties last,
Still let each following Day correct the last.

———

'T is a well spent penny that saves a groat.

Many Foxes grow grey, but few grow good.

Presumption first blinds a Man, then sets him a running.

APRIL

LIFE is a shelvy Sea, the Passage fear,
And not without a skilful Pilot steer.
Distrust thy Youth, experienc'd Age implore,
And borrow all the Wisdom of Threescore.
But chief a Father's, Mother's Voice revere;
'T is Love that chides, 't is Love that counsels here.
Thrice happy is the Youth, whose pliant Mind
To all a Parent's Culture is resign'd.

—

A cold April, The Barn will fill.

Content makes poor men rich; Discontent makes
rich Men poor.

Too much plenty makes Mouth dainty.

MAY

O, well begun, Virtue's great Work pursue,
Passions at first we may with Ease subdue;
But if neglected, unrestrain'd too long,
Prevailing in their Growth, by Habit Strong,
They've wrapp'd the Mind, have fix'd the stubborn
    Bent,
And Force of Custom to wild Nature lent;
Who then would set the crooked Tree aright,
As soon may wash the tawny Indian white.

—

If Passion drives, let Reason hold the Reins.

Neither trust, nor contend, nor lay wagers, nor lend;
And you'll have peace to your Lives end.

Drink does not drown Care, but waters it, and makes
it grow faster.

Who dainties love, shall Beggars prove.

JUNE

Industry's bounteous Hand may *Plenty* bring,
But wanting *frugal Care,* 't will soon take wing.
Small thy Supplies, and scanty in their Source,
'Twixt *Av'rice* and Profusion steer thy Course.
Av'rice is deaf to Want's Heart-bursting Groan,
Profusion makes the Beggar's Rags thy own:
Close Fraud and Wrong from griping Av'rice grow,
From rash *Profusion* desp'rate Acts and Woe.
A Man has no more Goods than he gets Good by.
Welcome, Mischief, if thou comest alone.

—

Different Sects like different clocks, may be all near
the matter, 'tho they don't quite agree.

JULY

Honour the softer Sex; with courteous Style,
And Gentleness of Manners, win their Smile;
Nor shun their virtuous Converse; but when Age
And Circumstance consent, thy Faith engage
To some discreet, well-natur'd, chearful Fair,
One not too stately for the Household Care,
One form'd in Person and in Mind to please,
To season Life, and all its Labours ease.

—

If your head is wax, don't walk in the Sun.

Pretty & Witty will wound if they hit ye.

Having been poor is no shame, but being ashamed of
it, is.

AUGUST

Gaming, the Vice of Knaves and Fools, detest,
Miner of Time, of Substance and of Rest;
Which, in the Winning or the Losing Part,
Undoing or undone, will wring the Heart:
Undone, self-curs'd, thy Madness thou wilt rue;
Undoing, Curse of others will pursue
Thy hated Head. A Parent's, Household's Tear,
A Neighbour's Groan, and *Heav'n's* displeasure fear.

—

'T is a laudable Ambition, that aims at being better than his Neighbours.

The wise Man draws more Advantage from his Enemies, than the Fool from his Friends.

SEPTEMBER

Wouldst thou extract the purest Sweet of Life,
Be nor Ally nor Principal in Strife.
A Mediator there, thy Balsam bring,
And lenify the Wound, and draw the Sting;
On *Hate* let *Kindness* her warm Embers throw,
And mould into a Friend the melting Foe.
The weakest Foe boasts some revenging Pow'r;
The weakest Friend some serviceable Hour.

—

All would live long, but none would be old.

Declaiming against Pride, is not always a Sign of Humility.

Neglect kills Injuries, Revenge increases them.

OCTOBER

In Converse be reserv'd, yet not morose,
In Season grave, in Season, too, jocose.
Shun Party-Wranglings, mix not in Debate
With Bigots in Religion or the State.
No Arms to Scandal or Detraction lend,
Abhor to wound, be fervent to defend.
Aspiring still to know, a Babbler scorn,
But watch where Wisdom opes her golden Horn.

—

9 Men in 10 are suicides.

Doing an Injury puts you below your Enemy; Revenging one makes you but even with him; Forgiving it sets you above him.

NOVEMBER

In quest of Gain be just: A Conscience clear
Is Lucre, more than Thousands in a Year;
Treasure no Moth can touch, no Rust consume;
Safe from the Knave, the Robber, and the Tomb.
Unrighteous Gain is the curs'd Seed of Woe,
Predestin'd to be reap'd by them who sow;
A dreadful Harvest! when th' avenging Day
Shall like a Tempest, sweep the Unjust away.

—

Most of the Learning in use, is of no great Use.

Great Good-nature, without Prudence, is a great
Misfortune.

Keep Conscience clear, Then never fear.

DECEMBER

But not from Wrong alone thy Hand restrain,
The *Appetite* of Gold demands the Rein.
What Nature asks, what Decency requires,
Be this the Bound that limits thy Desires:
This, and the gen'rous godlike Pow'r to feed
The Hungry, and to warm the Loins of *Need:*
To dry Misfortune's Tear, and scatter wide
Thy Blessings, like the Nile's o'erflowing Tide.

———

A man in a Passion rides a mad Horse.

Reader farewel, all Happiness attend thee; May each New-Year, better and richer find thee.

How to Get Riches

The Art of getting Riches consists very much in THRIFT. All Men are not equally qualified for getting Money, but it is in the Power of every one alike to practice this Virtue.

He that would be beforehand in the World, must be beforehand with his Business: It is not only ill Management, but discovers a slothful Disposition, to do that in the Afternoon, which should have been done in the Morning.

Useful Attainments in your Minority will procure Riches in Maturity, of which Writing and Accounts are not the meanest.

Learning, whether Speculative or Practical, is, in Popular or Mixt Governments, the Natural Source of Wealth and Honour.

PRECEPT I

In Things of moment, on thy self depend,
Nor trust too far thy Servant or thy Friend:
With private Views, thy Friend may promise fair,
And Servants very seldom prove sincere.

PRECEPT II

What can be done, with Care perform to Day,
Dangers unthought-of will attend Delay;
Your distant Prospects all precarious are,
And Fortune is as fickle as she's fair.

PRECEPT III

Nor trivial Loss, nor trivial Gain despise;
Molehills, if often heap'd, to Mountains rise:
Weigh every small Expence, and nothing waste,
Farthings long sav'd, amount to Pounds at last.

Poor RICHARD improved:

BEING AN

ALMANACK

AND

EPHEMERIS

OF THE

Motions of the SUN and MOON,

THE TRUE

Places and Aspects of the Planets;

THE

RISING and *SETTING* of the *SUN*;

AND THE

Rising, Setting *and* Southing *of the* Moon,

FOR THE

YEAR of our LORD 1756:

Being *Biſſextile* or LEAP-YEAR.

Containing alſo,

The Lunations, Conjunctions, Eclipſes, Judgment of the Weather, Riſing and Setting of the Planets, Length of Days and Nights, Fairs, Courts, Roads, &c. Together with uſeful Tables, chronological Obſervations, and entertaining Remarks.

Fitted to the Latitude of Forty Degrees, and a Meridian of near five Hours Weſt from *London* ; but may, without ſenſible Error, ſerve all the NORTHERN COLONIES.

By *RICHARD SAUNDERS*, Philom.

PHILADELPHIA:

Printed and Sold by B. FRANKLIN, and D. HALL.

COURTEOUS READER,

I suppose my Almanack may be worth the Money thou hadst paid for it, hadst thou no other Advantage from it, than to find the *Day of the Month*, the *remarkable Days*, the *Changes of the Moon*, the *Sun and Moons Rising and Setting*, and to foreknow the *Tides* and the *Weather*; these, with other Astronomical Curiosities, I have yearly and constantly prepared for thy Use and Entertainment, during now near two Revolutions of the Planet *Jupiter*. But I hope this is not all the Advantage thou hast reaped; for with a View to the Improvement of thy Mind and thy Estate, I have constantly interspers'd in every little Vacancy, *Moral Hints, Wise Sayings, and Maxims of Thrift*, tending to impress the Benefits arising from *Honesty, Sobriety, Industry* and *Frugality*; which if those hast duly observed, it is highly probably thou art *wiser* and *richer* many fold more than the Pence my Labours have cost thee. Howbeit, I shall not therefore raise my Price because thou art better able to pay; but being thankful for past Favours, shall endeavor to make my little Book more worthy thy Regard, by adding to those *Recipes* which were intended to *Cure the Mind*, some valuable Ones regarding the *Health of the Body*. They are recommended by the skilful, and by successful Practice. I wish a Blessing may attend the Use of them, and to thee all Happiness, being

Thy obliged Friend,
R. Saunders.

JANUARY

ASTRONOMY, hail, Science heavenly born!
Thy Schemes, the Life assist, the Mind adorn.
To changing Seasons give determin'd Space,
And fix to Hours and Years their measur'd Race
The point'ng *Dial,* on whose figur'd Plane,
Of Times still Flight we Notices obtain;
The *Pendulum,* dividing lesser Parts,
Their Rise acquire from thy inventive Arts.

—

A Change of Fortune hurts a wise Man no more
than a Change of the Moon.

FEBRUARY

Th' acute *Geographer*, th' *Historian* sage
By thy Discov'ries clear the doubtful Page
From marked Eclipses, *Longitude* perceive,
Can settle *Distances*, and Æra's give.
From his known Shore the Seaman distant far,
Steers safely guided by thy *Polar Star*;
Nor errs, when Clouds and Storms obscure its Ray,
His Compass marks him as exact a Way.

—

Does Mischief, Misconduct, and Warning displease
ye; Think there's a Providence 't will make ye easy.

Mine is better than Ours.

MARCH

When frequent Travels had th' instructive Chart
Supply'd the Prize of Philosophic Art!
Two curious mimic Globes, to Crown the Plan,
Were form'd; by his CREATOR's Image, Man.
The First, with Heav'ns bright Constellation vast,
Rang'd on the Surface, with th' Earth's Climes the last
Copy of this by human Race possest
Which Lands indent, and spacious Seas invest.

———

Love your Enemies, for they tell you your Faults.

He that has a Trade has an Office of Profit and
Honour.

The Wit of Conversation consists more in finding it in
others, than shewing a great deal yourself. He who goes
out of your Company pleased with his own Facetious-
ness and Ingenuity, will the sooner come into it again.
Most men had rather *please* than *admire* you, and seek less
to be *instructed* and *diverted,* than *approved* and *applauded,*
and it is certainly the most delicate Sort of Pleasure, to
please another.

But that sort of *Wit*, which employs itself insolently in Criticizing and Censuring, the Words and Sentiments of others in Conversation, is absolute *Folly*; for it answers none of the Ends of Conversation. He who uses it neither *improves others*, is *improved* himself, or pleases any one.

APRIL

Fram'd on imaginary Poles to move,
With Lines and different Circles mark'd above,
The pleasur'd Sense, by this Machine can tell,
In what Position various Nations dwell:
Round the wide Orb's exterior Surface spread;
How side-ways some the solid Convex tread:
While a more sever'd Race of busy Pow'rs
Project, with strange Reverse, their Feet to ours.

———

Be civil to all; sociable to many; familiar with few;
Friend to one; enemy to none.

Vain-glory flowereth, but beareth no Fruit.

As I spent some Weeks last Winter, in visiting my old
Acquaintance in the *Jerseys,* great Complaints I heard for
Want of money, and that leave to make more Paper Bills
could not be obtained. *Friends and Countrymen,* my Advice on this Head shall cost you nothing, and if you will
not be angry with me for giving it, I promise you not to
be offended if you do not take it.

You spend yearly at least *two hundred thousand pounds,* it
is said, in European, East-Indian and West-Indian com-
modities. Supposing one half of this expense to be in *things
absolutely necessary,* the other half may be called *superfluities,*
or, at best, conveniences, which, however, you might live

without for one little year, and not suffer exceedingly. Now to save this half, observe these few directions;

1. When you incline to have new clothes, look first well over the old ones, and see if you cannot shift with them another year, either by scouring, mending, or even patching if necessary. Remember, a patch on your coat, and money in your pocket, is better and more creditable, than a writ on your back, and no money to take it off.

2. When you incline to buy China ware, Chinces, India silks, or any other of their flimsy, slight manufactures, I would not be so hard with you, as to insist on your absolutely *resolving against it*; all I advise is, to *put it off* (as you do your repentance) *till another year*, and this, in some respects, may prevent an occasion for repentance.

3. If you are now a drinker of punch, wine or tea, twice a day, for the ensuing year drink them but once a day. If you now drink them but once a day, do it but every other day. If you now do it but once a week, reduce the practice to once a fortnight. And, if you do not exceed in quantity as you lessen the times, half your expense in these articles will be saved.

4. When you incline to drink rum, fill the glass *half* with water.

Thus at the year's end, there will be a *hundred thousand pounds* more money in your country.

If paper money in ever so great a quantity could be made, no man could get any of it without giving something for it. But all he saves in this way, will be *his own for nothing,* and his country actually so much richer. Then the merchant's old and doubtful debts may be honestly paid off, and trading become surer thereafter, if not so extensive.

MAY

So on the Apple's smooth suspended Ball,
(If greater we may represent by small)
The swarming Flies their reptile Tribes divide,
And cling Antipodal on every side.
Hence pleasant Problems may the mind discern
Of ev'ry Soil their Length of Days to learn;
Can tell when round, to each fix'd Place, shall come
Faint Dawn, Meridian Light, or Midnight Gloom.

———

Laws too gentle are seldom obeyed; too severe, seldom executed.

Trouble springs from Idleness; Toil from Ease.

Love and be loved.

JUNE

These gifts to astronomic Art we owe,
Its Use extensive, yet its Growth by slow.
If back we look on ancient Sages Schemes,
They seem ridiculous as Childrens Dreams;
How shall the Church, that boasts unerring Truth,
Blush as the Raillery of each modern Youth.
When told her Pope, of Heresy arraign'd
The Sage, who Earth's Rotation once maintain'd?

—

A wise Man will desire no more than what he may get justly, use soberly, distribute chearfully and leave contentedly.

The diligent Spinner has a large Shift.

JULY

Vain *Epicurus,* and his frantic Class,
Misdeem'd our Globe a plane quadrangle Mass;
A fine romantic Terras, spread in Slate,
On central Pillars that support its Weight
Like *Indian Sophs,* who this terrestrial Mould
Affirm, four sturdy Elephants uphold.
The Sun, new every morn, flat, small of Size,
Just what it measures to the naked Eyes.

—

A false Friend and a Shadow attend only while the Sun shines.

To-morrow every Fault is to be amended; but that To-morrow never comes.

It is observable that God has often called Men to Places of Dignity and Honour, when they have been busy in the honest Employment of their Vocation. *Saul* was seeking his Father's Asses, and *David* keeping his Father's Sheep, when called to the kingdom. The Shepherds were feeding their Flocks, when they had their glorious Revelation. God called the four Apostles from their Fishery, and

Matthew from the Receipt of Custom; *Amos* from among the Horsemen of *Tekoah, Moses* from keeping *Jethro's* Sheep, *Gideon* from the *Threshing Floor,* etc. God never encourages Idleness, and despises not Persons in the meanest Employments.

AUGUST

As pos'd the *Stagyrite's* dark School appears,
Perplex'd with Tales devis'd of *Chrystal Spheres*
Strange *solid Orbs,* and *Circles* oddly fram'd
Who with Philosophy their Reveries nam'd.
How long did *Ptolmy's* dark Riddle spread
With Doubts deep puzzling each scholastic Head
Till, like the *Theban* wise in story fam'd,
COPERNICUS that *Sphynxian* Monster sham'd.

—

Plough deep while Sluggard sleep;
And you shall have Corn to sell and to keep.

He that sows Thorns should never go barefoot.

SEPTEMBER

He the true Planetary system taught,
Which the learn'd Samian first from Egypt brought;
Long from the World conceal'd, in Error lost,
Whose rich Recovery latest Times shall boast.
Then TYCHO rose, who with incessant Pains,
In their due Ranks, replac'd the stony Trains
His Labours by fresh Industry mov'd,
Helvelius, Flamstead, Halley, since improv'd.

—

Laziness travels so slowly that Poverty soon overtakes him.

Sampson with his strong Body, had a weak Head, or he would not have laid it in a Harlot's lap.

OCTOBER

The *Lyncean* GALILEO then aspires
Thro' the rais'd Tube to mark the Stellar fires!
The *Gallaxy* with clustering Lights overspread,
The new-nam'd Stars in bright *Orions* Head,
The varying *Phases* circling Planets show
The *Solar Spots,* his Fame was first to know.
Of *Joves Attendants,* Orbs till then unknown,
Himself the big discovery claims alone.

———

When a Friend deals with a Friend, Let the bargain
be clear and well penn'd, That they may continue
Friends to the End.

He that never eats too much, will never be lazy.

NOVEMBER

Cassini next, and Huygens, like renown'd,
The *moons* and wondrous *Ring* of *Saturn* found
Sagacious KEPLER, still advancing saw
The *elliptic motion,* Natures plainest Law,
That Universal acts thro' every Part.
This laid the Basis of *Newtonian* Art.
NEWTON! vast mind! whose piercing Pow'rs apply'd
The secret Cause of Motion first descry'd;
Found Gravitation was the primal Spring
That wheel'd the Planets round their central King.

—

To be proud of Knowledge, is to be blind with Light;
To be proud of Virtue, is to poison yourself with the
Antidote.

Get what you can, and what you get, hold;
Tis the Stone that will turn all your Lead into Gold.

There is really a great Difference in Things some-
times where there seems to be but little Distinction in
Names. The *Man* of Honour is an internal, the *Person* of
Honour an external, the one a real, the other a fictitious,
Charactor. A *Person* of Honour may be a profane Liber-
tine, penurious, proud, may insult his inferiors, and de-

fraud his Creditors; but it is impossible for a *Man* of Honour to be guilty of any of these. The *Person* of Honour may flatter for Court Favours, or cringe for Popularity; he may be *for* or *against* his Country's Good, as it suits his private Views. But the *Man* of Honour can do none of these.

DECEMBER

Mysterious Impulse! that more clear to know
Exceeds the finite Reach of Art below.
Forbear, bold mortal! 't is an impious Aim
Own God immediate acting thro' the frame.
Tis He, unsearchable, in all resides;
He the FIRST CAUSE their Operations guides
Fear on his awful Privacy to press
But, honouring HIM, thy Ignorance confess.

—

An honest Man will receive neither Money nor
Praise that is not his due.

Saying and Doing have quarrel'd and parted.

Tell me my Faults, and mend your own.

Well, my friend, thou art just entering the last Month
of another year. If thou art a Man of Business, and of
prudent Care, be like thou wilt now settle thy accounts,
to satisfy thyself whether thou has gain'd or lost in the
Year past, and how much of either, the better to regulate
thy future Industry or thy common Expenses. This is
commendable—But it is not all.—Wilt thou not exam-

ine also thy *moral* Accompts, and see what improvements thou hast made in the Conduct of Life, what Vice subdued, what Virtue acquired; how much *better,* and how much wiser, as well as how much richer thou art grown? What shall it *profit* a Man, if he *gain* the whole World, but *lose* his own Soul. Without some Care in this Matter, tho' thou may'st come to count thy thousands, thou wilt possibly still appear poor in the Eyes of the Discerning, even *here,* and be really so for ever *hereafter.*

Poor RICHARD improved:

BEING AN

ALMANACK

AND

EPHEMERIS

OF THE

MOTIONS of the SUN and MOON;

THE TRUE

PLACES and ASPECTS of the PLANETS;

THE

RISING and *SETTING* of the *SUN*;

AND THE

Rising, Setting *and* Southing *of the* Moon,

FOR THE

YEAR of our LORD 1 7 5 7:

Being the First after LEAP-YEAR.

Containing also,

The Lunations, Conjunctions, Eclipses, Judgment of the Weather, Rising and Setting of the
Planets, Length of Days and Nights, Fairs, Courts,
Roads, &c. Together with useful Tables, chronological Observations, and entertaining Remarks.

Fitted to the Latitude of Forty Degrees, and a Meridian of near
five Hours West from *London*; but may, without sensible Error,
serve all the NORTHERN COLONIES.

By *RICHARD SAUNDERS*, Philom.

PHILADELPHIA:

Printed and Sold by B. FRANKLIN, and D. HALL.

COURTEOUS READER,

As no temporal Concern is of more Importance to us than Health, and that depends so much on the Air we every Moment breathe, the Choice of a good wholesome Situation to fix a Dwelling in, is a very serious Affair to every Countryman about to begin the World, and well worth his Consideration, especially as not only the Comfort of Living, but even the Necessaries of Life, depend in a great Measure upon it; since a Family frequently sick can rarely if ever thrive.... The following Extracts therefore from a late Medical Writer, Dr. Pringle, on that Subject, will, I hope, be acceptable and useful to some of my Readers.

I hear that some have already, to their great Advantage, put in Practice the Use of Oxen recommended in my last.... 'T is a Pleasure to me to be in any way serviceable in communicating useful Hints to the Publick; and I shall be obliged to others for affording me the Opportunity of enjoying that Pleasure more frequently, by sending me from time to time such of their own Observations, as may be advantageous if published in the Almanack.

I am thy obliged Friend,
RICHARD SAUNDERS.

How to make a STRIKING SUNDIAL, by which not only a Man's own Family, but all his Neighbours for ten Miles round, may know what a Clock it is, when the Sun shines, without seeing the Dial.

Chuse an open Place in your Yard or Garden, on which the Sun may shine all Day without any Impediment from Trees or Buildings. On the Ground mark out your Hour Lines, as for a horizontal Dial, according to Art, taking Room enough for the Guns. On the Line for One o'Clock, place one Gun; on the Two o'Clock Line two Guns, and so of the rest. The Guns must all be charged with Powder, but Ball is unnecessary. Your Gnomon or Style must have twelve burning Glasses annex't to it, and be so placed that the Sun shining through the Glasses, one after the other, shall cause the Focus or burning Spot to fall on the Hour Line of One, for Example, at One a Clock, and there kindle a Train of Gunpowder that shall fire one Gun. At Two a Clock, a Focus shall fall on the Hour Line of Two, and kindle another Train that shall discharge two Guns successively: and so of the rest.

Note, There must be 78 Guns in all. Thirty-two Pounders will be best for this Use; but 18 Pounders may do, and will cost less, as well as use less Powder, for nine Pounds of Powder will do for one Charge of each eighteen Pounder, whereas the Thirty-two Pounders would require for each Gun 16 Pounds.

Note also, That the chief Expense will be the Powder, for the Cannon once bought, will, with Care, last 100 Years.

Note moreover, that there will be a great Saving of Powder in Cloudy Days.

Kind Reader, Methinks I hear thee say, That is indeed a good Thing to know how the Time passes, but this Kind of Dial, notwithstanding the mentioned Savings, would be very Expensive; and the Cost greater than the Advantage, Thou art wise, my Friend, to be so considerate beforehand; some Fools would not have found out so much, till they had made the Dial and try'd it.... Let all such learn that many a private and many a publick Project, are like this Striking Dial, great Cost for little Profit.

JANUARY

CONVERSATION HINTS

Good Sense and Learning may Esteem obtain.
Humor and Wit a Laugh, if rightly ta'en;
Fair Virtue Admiration may impart;
But 't is GOOD-NATURE only wins the Heart;
It moulds the Body to an easy Grace,
And brightens every Feature of the Face;
It smooths th' unpolished Tongue with Eloquence,
And adds Persuasion to the finest Sense.

———

He that would rise at Court, must begin by creeping.

Many a Man's own Tongue gives Evidence against
his Understanding.

Nothing dries sooner than a Tear.

FEBRUARY

Would you both please, and be instructed too,
The pride of shewing forth yourself subdue.
Hear every Man upon his fav'rite Theme
And ever be more knowing than you seem.
The lowest Genius will afford some Light,
Or give a Hint that had escaped your Sight.
Doubt, till he thinks you on Conviction yield,
And with fit Questions let each Pause be fill'd.
And the most knowing will with Pleasure grant,
You're rather much reserv'd than ignorant.

—

'T is easier to build two Chimneys than maintain one in Fuel.

Anger warms the Invention, but overheats the Oven.

Rules of Law Fit to be Observed in Purchasing

From an old Book

First, see the Land which thou intend'st to buy
Within the Sellers title clear doth lie.
And that no Woman to it doth lay claim
By Dowry, Jointure, or some other Name.
That it may cumber. Know if bound or free
The Tenure stand, and that from each Feoffee
It be released: That the Seller be so old
That he may lawful sell, thou lawful hold.
Have special Care that it not mortgag'd lie,
Nor be entailed on Posterity.
Then if it stand in Statute bound or no:
Be well advised what Quit Rent out must go;
What Custom, Service hath been done of old,
By those who formerly the same did hold,
And if a wedded Woman put to Sale,
Deal not with her, unless she bring her Male.
For she doth under Covert-Baron go,
Altho' sometimes some also traffick so.
Have special Care to make thy Charter run
To thee, thine Heirs, Executors, Assigns,
For that beyond thy Life securely binds.

These Things forknown and done, you may prevent
Those Things rash Buyers many times repent.
And yet, when as you have done all you can
If you'd be sure, deal with an honest Man.

Very good Rules, these, and sweetly sung. If they are learnt by heart, and repeated often to keep them in Memory, they may happen to save the Purchaser more Pence than the Price of my Almanack. In Imitation of this old Writer, I have thoughts of turning Coke's Institutes, and all our Province Laws into Metre, hoping thereby to engage some of our young Lawyers and old Justices to read a little.

It is generally agreed to be Folly, to hazard the loss of a Friend, rather than to lose a Jest. But few consider how easily a Friend may be thus lost. Depending on the known Regard their Friends have for them, Jesters take more Freedom with Friends than they would dare to do with others, little thinking how much deeper we are wounded by an Affront from one we love. But the strictest Intimacy can never warrant Freedoms of this Sort; and it is indeed preposterous to think they should; unless we can suppose Injuries are less Evils when they are done to us by Friends, than when they come from other Hands.

MARCH

The Rays of Wit gild wheresoe'er they strike,
But are not therefore fit for all alike;
They charm the lively, but the grave offend
And raise a Foe as often as a Friend;
Like the resistless Beams of blazing Light,
That cheer the strong, and pain the weekly sight.
If a bright Fancy therefore be your Share
Let Judgment watch it with a Guardian's care.

—

It is Ill-manners to silence a Fool, and Cruelty to let him go on.

Scarlet, Silk and Velvet have put out the Kitchen Fire.

APRIL

'T is like a Torrent, apt to overflow,
Unless by constant Government kept low;
And ne'er inefficacious passes by,
But overturns or gladdens all that's nigh.
Or else, like Trees, when suffer'd wild to shoot,
That put forth much, but all unripen'd Fruit;
It turns to Affection and Grimace,
As like to Wit as Gravity to Grace.

—

He that would catch Fish, must venture his Bait.

Men take more pains to mask than mend.

One To-day is worth two To-morrows.

MAY

How hard soe'er it be to bridle Wit,
Yet Mem'ry oft no less requires the Bit:
How many, hurried by its Force away,
For ever in the Land of Gossips stay!
Usurp the Province of the Nurse, to lull,
Without her Privilege for being dull!
Tales upon Tales they raise, ten Stories high,
Without Regard to Use or Symmetry.

———

The way to be safe, is never to be secure.

Dally not with other Folks Women or Money.

Work as if you were to live 100 years, Pray as if you were to die To-morrow.

JUNE

A Story should, to please, at least seem true,
Be apropos, well told, concise, and new;
And whensoe'er it deviates from these Rules,
The Wise will sleep, and leave Applause to Fools.
But others, more intolerable yet,
The Waggeries that they've said, or heard, repeat
Heavy by Mem'ry made, and what's the worst,
At second-hand as often as at first.

———

Pride breakfasted with Plenty, dined with Poverty, supped with Infamy.

Retirement does not always secure Virtue; Lot was upright in the City; wicked in the Mountain.

Excess of Wit may oftentimes beguile:
Jests are not always pardon'd ... by a Smile.
Men may disguise their Malice at the Heart,
And seem at Ease ... tho' pain'd with inward Smart.
Mistaken, we ... think all such Wounds of course
Reflection cures; ... alas! it makes them worse.
Like Scratches they with double Anguish seize.
Rankle with Time, and fester by Degrees.

But sarcastical Jests on a Man's Person or his Manners, tho' hard to bear, are perhaps more easily borne than those that touch his Religion. Men are generally warm in what regards their religious Tenets, either from a Tenderness of Conscience, or a high Sense of their own Judgements. People of plain Parts and honest Dispositions, look on Salvation as too serious a Thing to be jested with; and Men of speculative Religion, who profess from the Conviction rather of their Heads than Hearts, are not a bit less vehement than the real Devotees. He who says a slight or a severe Thing of their Faith, seems to them to have thereby undervalued their Understanding, and will consequently incur their Aversion, which no Man of common Sense would hazard, for a lively Expression; much less a person of good Breeding, who should make it his chief Aim to be well with all.

Like some grave Matron of a noble Line,
With awful Beauty does Religion shine.
Just Sense should teach us to reverse the Dame,
Nor, by imprudent Jests, to spot her Fame.
In common Life you'll own this Reas'ning right,
That none but Fools in gross Abuse delight:
Then use it here ... nor think the Caution vain,
To be polite, Men need not be profane.

JULY

But above all Things, raillery decline,
Nature but few does for that Talk design;
'T is in the ablest Hand a dangerous Tool,
But never fails to wound the meddling Fool;
For all must grant it needs no common Art
To keep Men patient while we make them smart.
Not Wit alone, nor Humour's self, will do,
Without Good-nature, and much Prudence too.

—

Idleness is the Dead Sea, that swallows all Virtues:
Be active in Business, that Temptation may miss her
Aim; The Bird that sits, is easily shot.

Shame and the Dry-belly-ach were Diseases of the
last Age, this seems to be cured of them.

AUGUST

Of all the Qualities that help to raise
In Men, the Universal Voice of Praise,
Whether in Pleasure or in Use they end,
There's none that can with MODESTY contend.
Yet 't is but little that its Form be caught,
Unless its Origin be first in Thought;
Else rebel Nature will reveal the Cheat,
And the whole Work of Art at once defeat.

—

Tho' the Mastiff be gentle, yet bite him not by the Lip.

Great Alms giving, lessen no Man's living.

The Royal Crown cures not the Head-ach.

ON THE FREEDOM OF THE PRESS

While free from Force the Press remains,
Virtue and Freedom chear our Plains,
And Learning Largesses bestows,
And keeps unlicens'd open House.
We to the Nation's publick Mart
Our Works of Wit, and Schemes of Art,
And philosophic Goods, this Way,
Like Water carriage, cheap convey.
This Tree which Knowledge so affords,
Inquisitors with flaming Swords
From Lay-Approach with Zeal defend,
Lest their own Paradise should end.

   The Press from her fecundous Womb
Brought forth the Arts of Greece and Rome;
Her offspring, skill'd in Logic War,
Truth's Banner wav'd in open Air;
The Monster Superstition fled,
And hid in Shades her Gorgon Head;
And awless Pow'r, the long kept Field,
By Reason quell'd, was forc'd to yield.

This Nurse of Arts, and Freedom's Fence,
To chain, is Treason against Sense:
And Liberty, thy thousand Tongues
None silence who design no Wrongs;
For those who use the Gag's Restraint,
First Rob, before they stop Complaint.

SEPTEMBER

Hold forth upon yourself on no Pretence,
Unless invited, or in Self-Defence;
The Praise you take, altho' it be your Due,
Will be suspected if it come from you,
If to seem modest, you some faults confess,
The World suspect yet more, and never less:
For each Man, by Experience taught, can tell
How strong a Flatterer does within him dwell.

—

Act uprightly and despise Calumny; Dirt may stick
to a Mud Wall, but not to polish'd Marble.

OCTOBER

No part of Conduct asks for Skill more nice,
Tho' none more common, than to give Advice:
Misers themselves, in this will not be saving,
Unless their Knowledge makes it worth the having.
And Where's the Wonder, when we will intrude,
An useless Gift, it meets Ingratitude?
Shun then, unask'd, this arduous Task to try;
But, if consulted, use Sincerity.

—

The Borrower is a Slave to the Lender; the Security to both.

Singularity in the right, hath ruined many: Happy those who are convinced of the general Opinion.

NOVEMBER

Be rarely warm in Censure or in Praise;
Few Men deserve our Passion either ways:
For half the World but floats 'twixt Good and Ill,
As Chance disposes Objects, these the Will;
'T is but a see-saw Game, where Virtue now
Mounts above Vice, and then sinks down as low.
Besides, the Wise still hold it for a Rule,
To trust that Judgment most, that seems most cool.

———

Proportion your Charity to the strength of your Estate, or God will Proportion your Estate to the Weakness of your Charity.

The Tongue offends and the Ears get the Cuffing.

Some antient Philosophers have said, that Happiness depends more on the inward Disposition of Mind than on outward Circumstances; and that he who cannot be happy in any State, can be so in no State. To be happy, they tell us we must be content. Right. But they do not teach us how we may become content. Poor Richard shall give you a short good Rule for that. To be content look backward on those who possess less than yourself, not forward on those who possess more. If this does not make you content, you don't deserve to be happy.

CONTENTMENT! Parent of Delight,
So much a stranger to our Sight.
Say, Goddess, in what happy Place
Mortals behold thy blooming Face;
Thy gracious Auspices impart,
And for thy Temple chuse my Heart.
They whom thou deignest to inspire,
Thy Science learn, to bound Desire;
By happy Alchymy of Mind
They turn to Pleasure all they find.
Unmov'd when the rude Tempest blows,
Without an Opiate they repose;
And, cover'd by your Shield, defy
The whizzing Shafts that round them fly;
Nor, meddling with the Gods Affairs,
Concern themselves with distant Cares;
But place their Bliss in mental Rest,
And feast upon the Good possest.

DECEMBER

Would you be well receiv'd where'er you go,
Remember each Man vanquish'd is a Foe:
Resist not therefore to your utmost Might,
But let the Weakest think he's sometimes right;
He, for each Triumph you shall thus decline,
Shall give ten Opportunities to shine;
He sees, since once you owned him to excel,
That 't is his Interest you should reason well.

—

Sleep without Supping, and you'll rise without owing for it.

When other Sins grow old by Time,
Then Avarice is in its prime,
Yet feed the Poor at Christmas time.

Poor Richard improved:

BEING AN
ALMANACK
AND
EPHEMERIS

OF THE
MOTIONS of the SUN and MOON;
THE TRUE
PLACES and ASPECTS of the PLANETS;
THE
RISING and SETTING of the SUN;
AND THE
Rising, Setting and Southing of the Moon,
FOR THE
YEAR of our LORD 1758:
Being the Second after LEAP-YEAR.

Containing also,

The Lunations, Conjunctions, Eclipses, Judgment of the Weather, Rising and Setting of the Planets, Length of Days and Nights, Fairs, Courts, Roads, &c. Together with useful Tables, chronological Observations, and entertaining Remarks.

Fitted to the Latitude of Forty Degrees, and a Meridian of near five Hours West from *London*; but may, without sensible Error, serve all the NORTHERN COLONIES.

By *RICHARD SAUNDERS*, Philom.

PHILADELPHIA:
Printed and Sold by B. FRANKLIN, and D. HALL.

COURTEOUS READER,

I have heard that nothing gives an Author so great Pleasure, as to find his Works respectfully quoted by other learned Authors. This pleasure I have seldom enjoyed, for tho' I have been, if I may say it without Vanity, an *eminent Author* of Almanacks annually now a full quarter of a Century, my Brother Authors in the same Way, for what Reason I know not, have ever been very sparing in their Applauses; and no other Author has taken the least notice of me, so that did not my Writings produce me some solid *Pudding,* the great Deficiency of *Praise* would have quite discouraged me.

I concluded at length, that the People were the best Judges of my Merit; for they buy my Works; and besides, in my Rambles, where I am not personally known, I have frequently heard one or other of my Adages repeated, with *as Poor Richard says,* at the End on 't; this gave me some Satisfaction, as it showed not only that my Instructions were regarded, but discovered likewise some Respect for my Authority; and I own that to encourage the practice of remembering and repeating those wise Sentences, I have sometimes *quoted myself* with great gravity.

Judge then how much I must have been gratified by an Incident I am going to relate to you. I stopt my Horse lately where a great Number of people were collected at a Vendue, of Merchant Goods. The Hour of Sale not being come, they were conversing on the Badness of the Times, and one of the Company call'd to a plain clean old Man, with white Locks, *Pray Father* Abraham, *what think you of the Times? Won't these heavy Taxes quite ruin the Country? How shall we* BE EVER *able to pay them? What would you advise us to?*—Father *Abraham* stood up, and reply'd, If you'd have my Advice, I'll give it you in short, *for a Word to the Wise is enough, and many Words won't fill a Bushel, as Poor Richard says.* They join'd in desiring him to speak his Mind, and gathering round him, he proceeded as follows;

"Friends, says he, and Neighbours, the Taxes are indeed very heavy, and if those laid on by the Government were the only Ones we had to pay, we might more easily discharge them; but we have many others, and much more grievous to some of us. We are taxed twice as much by our *Idleness,* three times as much by our *Pride,* and four times as much by our *Folly,* and from these Taxes the Commissioners cannot ease or deliver us by allowing an Abatement. However let us hearken to good Advice, and something may be done for us; *God helps them that help themselves, as Poor Richard* says in his Almanack of 1733.

It would be thought a hard Government that should tax its People, one tenth Part of their *Time,* to be employed in its Service. But *Idleness* taxes many of us much more, if we reckon all that is spent in absolute *Sloth,* or doing of nothing with that which is spent in idle Employments or Amusements that amount to nothing. *Sloth, by bringing on Diseases absolutely shortens Life. Sloth, like Rust, consumes faster than Labour wears, while the used Key is always bright,* as *Poor Richard* says. But *dost thou love Life, then do not squander Time, for that's the Stuff Life is made of,* as *Poor Richard* says.—How much more than is necessary do we spend in Sleep! forgetting that *The Sleeping Fox catches no Poultry,* and that *there will be sleeping enough in the Grave,* as *Poor Richard* says. If Time be of all Things the most precious, *wasting of Time* must be, as *Poor Richard* says, *the greatest Prodigality,* since, as he elsewhere tells us, *Lost Time is never found again;* and what we call *Time-enough, always proves little enough.* Let us then be up and doing, and doing to the Purpose; so by Diligence shall we do more with less Perplexity. *Sloth makes all things difficult, but Industry all Things easy,* as *Poor Richard* says; and *He that riseth late, must trot all Day, and shall scarce overtake his Business at night.* While *Laziness travels so slowly, that Poverty soon overtakes him,* as we read in *Poor Richard,* who adds, *Drive thy Business, let not that drive thee; and Early to Bed, and early to rise, makes a Man healthy, wealthy, and wise.*

So what signifies *wishing* and *hoping* for better times. We may make these Times better if we bestir ourselves. *Industry need not wish* as *Poor Richard* says, and *He that lives upon Hope will die fasting. There are no Gains, without Pains;* then *Help Hands, for I have no Lands,* or if I have, they are smartly taxed. And as *Poor Richard* likewise observes, *He that hath a Trade hath an Estate*, and *He that hath a Calling hath an Office of Profit and Honour*; but then the *Trade* must be worked at, and the *Calling* well followed, or neither the *Estate*, nor the *Office*, will enable us to pay our Taxes.—If we are industrious we shall never starve; for as *Poor Richard* says, *At the working Man's House Hunger looks in, but dares not enter.* Nor will the Bailiff or the Constable enter, for *Industry pays Debts while Despair encreaseth them*, says *Poor Richard.*—What though you have found no Treasure, nor has any rich Relation left you a Legacy, *Diligence is the Mother of Good-luck*, as *Poor Richard* says, *and God gives all things to Industry.* Then *plough deep, while Sluggards sleep, and you shall have Corn to sell and to keep*, says *Poor Dick.* Work while it is called To-day, for you know not how much you may be hindered To-morrow, which makes *Poor Richard* say, *One To-day is worth two To-morrows*; and farther, *Have you somewhat to do To-morrow, do it to To-day.* If you were a Servant would you not be ashamed that a good Master should catch you idle? Are you then your own Master, *be ashamed to catch yourself idle*, as *Poor Dick* says. When there is so much to be done for yourself, your Family, your Country, and your gracious King, be up by Peep of Day; *Let not the Sun look down and say, Inglorious here he lies.* Handle your Tools without Mittens; remember that *the Cat in Gloves catches no Mice*, as *Poor Richard* says. 'T is true there is much to be done, and perhaps you are weak-handed, but stick to it steadily, and you will see great Effects, for *constant Dropping wears away Stones,* and by *Diligence and Patience, the Mouse ate in two the Cable;* and *little Strokes fell great Oaks,* as *Poor Richard* says in his Almanack, the Year I cannot just now remember.

Methinks I hear some of you say, *Must a Man afford himself no Leisure?*—I will tell thee My Friend, what *Poor Richard* says, *Employ thy Time well if thou meanest to gain Leisure;* and, *since thou art not sure of a Minute, throw not away an Hour.* Leisure is Time for doing something useful; this Leisure the diligent man will obtain, but the lazy man never; so that, as *Poor Richard* says, *a Life of Leisure and a Life of Laziness are two Things.* Do you imagine that Sloth will afford you more Comfort than Labour? No, for as *Poor Richard* says, *Trouble springs from Idleness, and grievous Toil from needless Ease. Many without Labour, would live by their* WITS *only, but they break for want of stock.* Whereas Industry gives Comfort, and Plenty and Respect: *Fly Pleasures and they'll follow you. The diligent Spinner has a large Shift; and now I have a Sheep and a Cow, every Body bids me Good morrow,* all which is well said by *Poor Richard.*

But with our Industry, we must likewise be *steady, settled,* and *careful,* and oversee our own Affairs *with our own Eyes,* and not trust too much to others; for, as *Poor Richard* says,

I never saw an oft removed Tree,
Nor yet an oft removed Family,
That throve so well as those that settled be.

And again, *Three Removes is as bad as a Fire;* and again, *Keep thy Shop, and thy Shop will keep thee;* and again, *If you would have your Business done, go; if not, send.* And again,

He that by the Plough must thrive,
Himself must either hold or drive.

And again, *The Eye of a Master will do more Work than both his Hands;* and again, *Want of Care does us more Damage than Want of Knowledge;* and again, *Not to oversee Workmen, is to leave them your Purse open.* Trusting too much to others Care is the Ruin of many; for, as the *Almanack* says, *In the Affairs of this World, Men are saved, not by Faith, but by the Want of it;* but a Man's own Care is profitable; for, saith *Poor Dick, Learning is to the Studious,* and *Riches to the Careful,* as well as *Power to the Bold,* and *Heaven to the Virtuous.* And, farther, *If you would have a faithful Servant, and one that you like, serve yourself.* And again, he adviseth to Circumspection and Care, even in the smallest Matters, because sometimes *a little Neglect may breed great Mischief,* adding, *for want of a Nail, the Shoe was lost; for want of a Shoe the Horse was lost; and for want of a Horse the Rider was lost,* being overtaken and slain by the Enemy, all for want of Care about a Horse-shoe Nail.

So much for Industry, my Friends, and Attention to one's own Business; but to these we must add *Frugality*, if we would make our *Industry* more certainly successful. A man may, if he knows not how to save as he gets, *Keep his Nose all his Life to the Grindstone*, and die not worth a *Groat* at last. *A fat Kitchen makes a lean Will, as Poor Richard says; and*

Many Estates are spent in the Getting,
Since Women for Tea forsook Spinning and Knitting,
And Men for Punch forsook Hewing and Splitting.

If you would be wealthy, says he, in another Almanack, *think of Saving, as well as of Getting: The* Indies *have not made* Spain *rich, because her* Outgoes *are greater than her* Incomes. Away then with your expensive Follies, you will not have so much cause to complain of hard Times, heavy Taxes, and chargeable Families; for as *Poor Dick* says,

Women and Wine, Game and Deceit,
Make the Wealth small and the Wants great.

And farther, *What maintains one Vice would bring up two Children.* You may think perhaps that a *little* Tea or a *little* Punch now and then, Diet a *little* more costly, Clothes a *little* finer, and a *little* Entertainment now and then, can be no *great* Matter; but remember what *Poor Richard* says, *Many* a Little *makes a Mickle;* and farther, *Beware* of little

Expenses; a small Leak will sink a great Ship; and again, *Who Dainties love shall Beggars prove;* and moreover, *Fools make Feasts and wise Men eat them.*

Here you are all got together at this Vendue of *Finerie* and *Knicknacks.* You call them *Goods,* but if you do not take Care, they will prove *Evils* to some of you. You expect they will be sold *cheap,* and perhaps they may for less than they cost; but if you have no Occasion for them, they must be *dear* to you. Remember what *Poor Richard* says, *Buy what thou hast no Need of, and ere long thou shalt sell thy Necessaries.* And again, *At a great Pennyworth pause a while:* He means, that perhaps the Cheapness is *apparent* only, and not *real;* or the Bargain, by straitning thee in thy Business, may do thee more Harm than Good. For in another Place he says, *Many have been ruined by buying good Pennyworths.* Again *Poor Richard* says, *'T is foolish to lay out Money in a Purchase of Repentance;* and yet this Folly is practised every Day at Vendues, for want of minding the Almanack. *Wise Men,* as *Poor Dick* says, *learn by others Harms, Fools scarcely by their own;* but *Felix quem faciunt aliena Pericula cautum.* Many a one, for the Sake of Finery on the Back, have gone with a hungry Belly, and half starved their Families; *Silks and Satins, Scarlet and Velvets,* as *Poor Richard* says, *put out the Kitchen Fire.* These are not the *Necessaries* of Life; they can scarcely be called the *Conveniences,* and yet only because they look pretty how many *want* to *have* them. The *artificial* Wants of

Mankind thus become more numerous than the *natural;* and as *Poor Dick* says, *For one* poor *Person there are an hundred* indigent. By these, and other Extravagancies, the Genteel are reduced to Poverty, and forced to borrow of those whom they formerly despised, but who through *Industry* and *Frugality* have maintained their Standing; in which case it appears plainly, that a *Ploughman on his Legs is higher than a Gentleman on his Knees,* as *Poor Richard* says. Perhaps they have had a small Estate left them, which they knew not the Getting of,—they think *'t is Day and will never be Night;* that a little to be spent out of *so much,* is not worth minding; (*a Child and a Fool,* as *Poor Richard* says, *imagine Twenty Shillings and Twenty Years can never be spent*) but, *always taking out of the Meat-tub and never putting in, soon comes to the Bottom;* then, as *Poor Dick* says, *When the Well's dry, they know the Worth of Water.* But this they might have known before, if they had taken his Advice; *If you would know the Value of Money, go and try to borrow some; for he that goes a borrowing goes a sorrowing;* and indeed so does he that lends to such People, when he goes *to get it in again.*—*Poor Dick* farther advises, and says,

Fond *Pride of Dress,* is sure a very Curse;
E'er *Fancy* you consult, consult your Purse.

And again, *Pride is as loud a Beggar as Want, and a great deal more saucy.* When you have bought one fine Thing you must buy ten more, that your appearance may be all of a Piece; but *Poor Dick* says, *'T is easier to* suppress *the first Desire, than to* satisfy *all that follow it.* And 't is as truly Folly for the Poor to ape the Rich, as for the Frog to swell, in order to equal the Ox.

> Great Estates may venture more,
> But little Boats should keep near Shore.

'T is however a Folly soon punished; for *Pride that dines on Vanity sups on Contempt,* as *Poor Richard* says. And in another Place, *Pride breakfasted with Plenty, dined with Poverty, and supped with Infamy.* And after all, of what Use is this *Pride of Appearance,* for which so much is risked, so much is suffered! It cannot promote Health, or ease Pain; it makes no Increase of Merit in the Person, creates Envy, it hastens Misfortune.

> What is a Butterfly? At best
> He's but a Caterpillar drest.
> The gaudy Fop's his Picture just.

as *Poor Richard* says.

But what Madness must it be to *run in Debt* for these Superfluities! We are offered by the Terms of this Vendue, *Six Months Credit;* and that perhaps has induced some of us to attend it, because we cannot spare the ready Money, and hope now to be fine without it. But, ah, think what you do when you run in Debt; *You give to another Power over your Liberty.* If you cannot pay at the Time, you will be ashamed to see your Creditor; you will be in Fear when you speak to him; you will make poor pitiful sneaking Excuses, and by Degrees come to lose your Veracity, and sink into base downright lying; for as *Poor Richard* says, *The second Vice is Lying, the first is running in Debt.* And again, to the same Purpose, *Lying rides upon Debt's Back.* Whereas a freeborn *Englishman* ought not to be ashamed or afraid to see or speak to any Man living. But Poverty often deprives a Man of all Spirit and Virtue; *'T is hard for an empty Bag to stand upright,* as *Poor Richard* truly says. What would you think of that Prince, or that Government, who should issue an Edict forbidding you to dress like a Gentleman, or a Gentlewoman, on Pain of Imprisonment or Servitude! Would you not say, that you are free, have a Right to dress as you please, and that such an Edict would be a Breach of your Privileges, and such a Government tyrannical! And yet you are about to put yourself under that Tyranny when you run in Debt for such Dress! Your Creditor has Authority at his Pleasure to deprive you of your Liberty, by confining you in Goal for Life, or to sell you for a Servant, if you should not be able to pay him! When you have got your Bargain, you may, perhaps, think little of Payment! but *Creditors, Poor Richard* tells us, *have better Memories than Debtors;* and in another Place says, *Creditors are a superstitious Sect, great Observers of set Days and Times.* The Day comes round before you are aware, and the Demand is made before you are prepared to satisfy it, Or if you bear your Debt in Mind, the Term which at first seemed so long, will, as it lessens, appear extremely short. *Time* will seem to have added Wings to his Heels as well as Shoulders. *Those have a short Lent,* saith *Poor Richard, who owe Money to be paid at Easter.* Then, since as he says, *The Borrower is a Slave to the Lender, and the Debtor is the Creditor,* disdain the Chain, preserve your Freedom; and maintain your Independency; Be *industrious* and *free;* be *frugal* and *free.* At present, perhaps, you may think yourself in thriving Circumstances, and that you can bear a little Extravagance without Injury; but,

> For Age and Want save while you may;
> No Morning Sun lasts a whole Day,

as *Poor Richard* says.—Gain may be temporary and uncertain, but ever while you live Experience is constant and certain; and *'t is easier to build two Chimnies than to keep one in Fuel,* as *Poor Richard* says. *So rather go to Bed supperless than rise in Debt.*

> Get what you can, and what you get hold.
> 'T is the stone that will turn all your Lead into Gold,

as *Poor Richard* says. And when you have got the Philosopher's Stone, sure you will no longer complain of the
bad Times, or the Difficulty of paying Taxes.

This Doctrine, my Friends, is *Reason* and *Wisdom;* but
after all, do not depend too much on your own *Industry,*
and *Frugality,* and *Prudence,* though excellent Things; for
they may all be blasted without the Blessing of Heaven;
and therefore ask that Blessing humbly, and be not un-
charitable to those that at present seem to want it, but
comfort and help them. Remember *Job* suffered and was
afterwards prosperous.

And now to conclude, *Experience keeps a dear School, but
Fools will learn in no other, and scarce in that;* for it is true, *we
may give Advice, but we cannot give Conduct,* as *Poor Richard*
says: However, remember this, *They that won't be coun-
selled, can't be helped,* as *Poor Richard* says: and farther, That
if you will not hear Reason, she'll surely wrap your Knuckles.

Thus the old Gentleman ended his Harangue. The
People heard it, and approved the Doctrine, and imme-
diately practised the contrary, just as if it had been a
common Sermon; for the Vendue opened, and they
began to buy extravagantly, notwithstanding all his Cau-
tions, and their own Fear of Taxes.—I found the good
Man had thoroughly studied my Almanacks, and di-
gested all I had dropt on those Topicks during the
Course of Five-and-Twenty Years. The frequent men-
tion he made of me must have tired any one else, but my

Vanity was wonderfully delighted with it, though I was conscious that not a tenth Part of this Wisdom was my own which he ascribed to me, but rather the *Gleanings* I had made of the Sense of all Ages and Nations. However, I resolved to be the better for the Echo of it; and though I had at first determined to buy Stuff for a new Coat, I went away resolved to wear my old one a little longer. *Reader,* if thou wilt do the same, thy Profit will be as great as mine.

> I am, as ever,
> Thine to serve thee,
> RICHARD SAUNDERS.

July 7, 1757.

JANUARY

ON AMBITION

I know, young Friend, Ambition fills your Mind,
And in Life's Voyage is th' impelling Wind;
But at the Helm let sober Reason stand
And steer the Bark with Heav'n-directed Hand:
So shall you safe *Ambitions* Gale receive,
And ride securely, tho' the Billows heave;
So shall you shun the giddy Hero's Fate,
And by her Influence be both good and great.

—

One Nestor is worth two Ajaxes.

When you're an Anvil, hold you still;
When you're a Hammer, strike your fill.

FEBRUARY

She bids you first, in Life's soft Vernal Hours,
With active Industry wake Natures Powers;
With rising Years, still rising Arts display,
With new-born Graces mark each new-born Day,
'T is now the Time young Passion to command
While yet the pliant Stem obeys the Hand;
Guide now the Courser with a steady rein
E'er yet he bounds o'er Pleasures flow'ry Plane;
In Passion's Strife, no Medium you can have;
You rule a Master, or submit a Slave.

—

When Knaves betray each other, one can scarce be blamed or the other pitied.

He that carries a small Crime easily, will carry it on when it comes to be an Ox.

MARCH

For whom these Toils, you may perhaps enquire;
First for *yourself,* next Nature will inspire,
The filial Thought, fond Wish, and Kindred Tear
Which makes the Parent and the Sister dear:
To these, in closest Bands of Love, ally'd,
Their Joy and Grief you live, their Shame or Pride;
Hence timely learn to make their Bliss your own,
And scorn to think or act for Self *alone.*

—

Happy Tom Crump ne'er sees his own Hump.

Fools need Advice most, but wise Men only are the
better for it.

APRIL

Hence bravely strive upon your own to raise
Their Honour, Grandeur, Dignity and Praise.
But wider far, beyond the narrow Bound
Of Family, *Ambition* searches round:
Searches to find the Friend's delightful Face,
The Friend at last demands the second place,
And yet beware; for most desire a Friend
From meaner Motives, not for Virtue's End.
There are, who with fond Favour's fickle Gale
Now sudden swell, and now contract their Sail.

—

Silence is not always a Sign of Wisdom, but Babbling
is ever a Folly.

Great Modesty often hides great Merit.

You may delay, but Time will not.

MAY

This Week devour, the next with sickening Eye
Avoid, and cast the sully'd Plaything by;
There are, who tossing in the Bed of Vice,
For Flattery's Opiate give the highest Price;
Yet from the saving Hand of Friendship turn,
Her Medicines dread, her generous Offers spurn.
Deserted Greatness! who but pities thee?
By crowds encompass'd, thou no friend canst see:

—

Virtue may not always make a Face handsome, but Vice will certainly make it ugly.

Prodigality of Time produces Poverty of Mind as well as of Estate.

JUNE

Or should kind Truth invade thy gentle Ear,
We pity still; for thou no Truth canst hear.
Ne'er grudg'd thy Wealth to swell an useless State,
Yet, frugal, deems th' Expence of Friends too great;
For Friends ne'er mixing in ambitions Strife,
For Friends, the richest Furniture of Life!

—

Be yours, my son, a nobler, higher Aim

Your Pride to burn with Friendship's sacred Flame;

Content is the Philosopher's Stone, that turns all it
touches into Gold.

He that's content hath enough.

He that complains has too much.

Pride gets into the Coach, and Shame mounts
behind.

JULY

By Virtue kindled, by like Manners fed,
By mutual Wishes, mutual Favours spread,
Increas'd with Years, by candid Truth refin'd
Pour all its boundless Ardours thro' your mind
By yours the care a chosen Band to gain;
With them to Glory's radiant Summit strain,
Aiding and aided each, while all contend
Who best, who bravest, shall assist his Friend.

—

The first Mistake in public Business, is the going into it.

Half the Truth is often a great Lie.

The Way to see by Faith is to shut the Eye of Reason.

The Morning Daylight appears plainer when you put out your Candle.

AUGUST

Thus still should private Friendships spread around,
Till in their joint Embrace the Publick's found,
The common Friend!—Then all her Good explore;
Explor'd, pursue with each unbiass'd Power
But chief the greatest should her Laws revere,
Ennobling Honours, which she bids them wear
Ambition fills with Charity the Mind,
And pants to be the Friend of all Mankind.

—

A full Belly makes a dull Brain.

The Muses starve in a Cook's Shop.

Spare and have is better than spend and crave.

Good-Will, like the Wind, floweth where it listeth.

SEPTEMBER

Her Country all beneath one ambient Sky
Whosoe'er beholds you radiant Orb on high,
To whom one Sun impartial gives the Day,
To whom the Silver Moon her milder Ray,
Whom the same Water, Earth, and Air sustain,
O'er whom one Parent-King extends his Reign
Are her compatriots all, by her belov'd,
In Nature near, tho' far by Space remov'd;
On common Earth, no Foreigner she knows;
No Foe can find, or none but Virtue's Foes:

—

The Honey is sweet, but the Bee has a Sting.

In a corrupt Age, the putting the World in order
would breed Confusion; then e'en mind your own
Business.

OCTOBER

Ready she stands her cheerful Aid to lend;
To Want and Woe an undemanded Friend.
Nor thus advances others Bliss alone;
But in the Way to theirs, still finds her own.
Their's is her own. What, should your Taper light
Ten Thousand, burns it to yourself less bright?
"Men are ungrateful."—Be they so that dare!
Is that the Giver's or Receiver's Care?

———

To serve the Publick faithfully, and at the same time
please it entirely is impracticable.

Proud Modern Learning despises the antient:
Schoolmen are now laught at by school-boys.

NOVEMBER

Oh! blind to Joys, that from true Bounty flow;
To think those e'er repent whose *Hearts* bestow!
Man to his Maker thus best Homage pays,
Thus peaceful walks thro' Virtues pleasing Ways
Her gentle Image on the Soul imprest,
Bids each tempestuous Passion leave the Breast
Hence with her livid Self-devouring Snakes
Pale Envy flies; her quiver Slander breaks:
Thus falls (dire Scourage of a distracted Age!)
The Knave-led, one ey'd Monster, Party Rage.

—

Men often mistake themselves, seldom forget themselves.

The idle Man is the Devil's Hireling, whose Livery is Rags, whose Diet and Wages are Famine and Diseases.

DECEMBER

Ambition jostles with her Friends no more;
Nor thirsts Revenge to drink a Brothers Gore;
Fiery Remorse no stinging Scorpions rears:
O'er trembling Guilt no falling Sword appears.
Hence Conscience, void of Blame, her Front erects,
Hence just Ambition boundless Splendors crown
And hence she calls Eternity her own.—

—

Rob not God, nor the Poor, lest thou ruin thyself;
The Eagle snatcht a Coal from the Altar, but it fired
her Nest.

With bounteous cheer
Conclude the Year.

A Note on the Type

The principal text of this Modern Library edition
was set in a digitized version of Janson,
a typeface that dates from about 1690 and was cut by Nicholas Kis, a
Hungarian working in Amsterdam. The original matrices have
survived and are held by the Stempel foundry in Germany.
Hermann Zapf redesigned some of the weights and sizes for Stempel,
basing his revisions on the original design.